NOTHING DIVINE HERE

Gloria Mindock

Gloria Mindock
4/7/10

U ŠOKU ŠTAMPA

Cetinje, Montenegro & Springfield, Virginia

Cover Art: B. A. Bosaiya
www.bosaiya.com

Cover Design: William J. Kelle

ISBN: 978-0-578-04760-7

Library of Congress Control Number: 2010900680

ACKNOWLEDGMENTS

"Pain," *Aitia*
"Blue Skies," *Arizona Mandala Magazine*
"Cold" and "The Scene of the Crucifixion," *Atelier*
"Bridge" and "White Sheet," *Blackbox*
"Tornado," *Bogg*
"Cut," *Context South*
"Beaten," *The Doomed City*
"Nothing Divine Here" and "Confidential Memo," *Fire*
"Empty Field" and "Water," *The Golpherwood Review*
"It Has to Be This Way," *Gypsy*
"Choir," *K*
"Images of Grave," *Kings Review*
"Saint of Hearts," *New World Poetry*
"Denied Emotion," *Noctiluca*
"Harvest," *Pass Port Journal*
"In Hell," *Phoebe*
"China," "Republic," and "Visiting Artyom," *Poesia*
"Alone" and "Doppelganger vii," *Poet Lore*
"Scorch," *Poetry Motel*
"Feast," *River Styx*
"Doppelganger iv," *ten: by: six:*
"Passion," *Tin Wreath*
"Cautionary," "Charade," "Buried Definition," "Rough-Edged,"
"Silence, and "Dog Dance," *Wilderness House Literary Review*
"Cautionary," *Wilderness House Literary Review Anthology, No. 2*

In Romania, translated into the Romanian by Flavia Cosma

"Quiet Sky," "Alone," "Water," "Denied Emotion," *Aurora*
"Doppelganger ii," "Doppelganger vi," and "Breathe," *Unu: Revista de Cultura*
"Denied Emotion" and "Quiet Sky," *Citadela*
"Suitcase" and "Silence," *Mumur of Voices* (Anthology)

Some of the poems in this volume can be found in my poetry collection in Romania, "*La Porţile Raiului*" (Ars Longa Press, 2010), translated by Flavia Cosma.

I would like to thank the Massachusetts Cultural Council for a poetry fellowship awarded by the Somerville Arts Council which provided funding for the completion of this work.

The *Doppelganger* poems were published in 1992 as a chapbook by S. Press. They were also the text for a theatre piece by the same name, produced by Theatre S. in 1987.

The *Oh Angel* poems were published in 2005 as a chapbook, *Oh Angel*, by U Šoku Štampa.

I would like to thank Flavia Cosma for writing the foreword to the book and for her friendship. It has meant so much to me. Much appreciation goes to Ioan Tepelea of Oradea, Romania, for publishing so many of my poems in the journal *UNU: Revista de Cultura* and in the anthology "Murmur of Voices." My gratitude to Svetlana Dobritachanin for publishing this book, the years and years of friendship, and the many laughs. They never stop. I can't thank my dear friend Catherine Sasanov enough for all her editing. Catherine has always been there for me in all aspects of my life. A huge thank you to Susan Tepper for all that she has done for me and being so supportive of my work. I am grateful to William J. Kelle, my partner and huge supporter, no matter what I do. My heartfelt thanks to Carl Phillips, Dzvinia Orlowsky, and Mark Fleckenstein. We workshopped many of these poems during the period that we edited the *Boston Literary Review/BLuR* together. Thank you to Afaa Michael Weaver, both for the blurb, but more importantly, for his friendship. Much appreciation as well to Doug Holder, who has been so supportive, and to the Bagel Bards for their camaraderie and wonderful Saturday mornings! I am grateful to William James Austin for being so supportive of my more experimental work and his friendship of many years. I am so appreciate to B. A. Bosaiya who graciously gave me permission to use the photo for the cover. It was exactly what I was looking for. Thank you! Finally, my gratitude to Jennifer Atkinson who accepted the poem "Feast" for *River Styx* many years ago. That belief in my work at the very beginning has always kept me going.

TABLE OF CONTENTS

PART IV

PART V

PART VI

Foreword by Flavia Cosma

Passionate and rebellious, **Gloria Mindock's** poetry jumps
forcefully from the page, grabs the reader by the collar of his coat
and holds and hangs on to his/her attention.

In unison with the poet's heart, the nature of things is in
big turmoil here, forever searching for the elusive *Divine Harmony*,
the only force capable of rearranging the world into one of love
and understanding.

In a perpetual state of sadness and grief, these poems
descend to the very core of the raw discourse of the soul, devoid of
artifice and pose. The stark simplicity of their statement disarms us
and leaves us vulnerable in front of the bitter reality of life.

"There are many rooms of sadness in
this world, I just happen to be
in one of them" declares the poet.

In an effort to absorb and express the complexities of life
and death, of human relations and of so many misunderstandings
governing our journey on earth, **Gloria Mindock** fights every
demon and every betraying angel in order to bring forth, and sort
out, with a unique gift of clarity, a wide array of feelings and mixed
tonalities of emotions.

"Come closer and speak to me.
I am not your enemy until
You kiss me."

Ever aware of the inexorable passing of time, **Gloria
Mindock** offers this chilling metaphysical reflection:

"Maybe death is just air and just maybe our decaying
bodies are solid earth for the insects, and love is
just a pact we have with dirt."

The poetic language of *Nothing Divine Here* is breathtaking; through
stunning metaphors and images we are constantly swept away and
carried into the magic realm of true Poetry:

"The trees have all grown thorns, and the
flowers are horizontal"...

or

"Each letter I
wrote was running
sweet of ravenous frenzy..."

Nothing Divine Here is a deeply moving and thought-provoking poetry collection. It takes the reader into **Gloria**'s inner world, which is forever confronting the outward one, a world where sadness and pain cohabit with death and loss, and why not, with an ultimate hope for happiness:

> *"To my astonishment, there was an altar for hearts,*
> *communion was weekly and somehow –*
> *someday a new love, which was an old love,*
> *would return."*

These poems have a way of holding the most truth in a disciplined, concise form, touching the heart, stirring the mind, reminding us about the divinity of being human and finally acknowledging in a simple, direct phrasing, the all encompassing presence of God:

> *"Someday, I will ask God to*
> *sing to me*
> *He will smile and change*
> *my touch*
> *into directions of green..."*

"Evil or good angels,
I don't know which,
hurled you into my soul."

Rafael Alberti

NOTHING DIVINE HERE

Gloria Mindock

For my dear friend
who is such an
inspiration for me + who
has always been my
favorite writer! Thanks for
being so supportive of my work.
You are the best!
Much love —
Glo

WATER

I realized one thing
about my life today
It doesn't matter
Years from now
the company I had, will
have ceased
This planet will stop
This universe
exiled

I don't dream anymore
I'm only a skeleton
thinking about water
cruelly hungering for a
harvest

My wandering eyes grow with
touch
My internal sensibilities are
like footprints
They only last until
the next rain
Water beware!
My mouth is thirsty
My lips are living

I want more than a proud
future
I want eternal fruitfulness
A voice with blue
A challenge with fertility
expanding into violet
opening up the unanswered

Hunt me out, death
I am nothing but a touch to
this day, a memory of night,
and bread for some other secret

PART I

SUITCASE

What shall be packed in my
suitcase when I leave?…
Fairy tales for a life not
lived right.
A whole life of occasional
hearts shoved into a box with
locks. I'm the only one with the
exact memories of all the men I loved.

In one sentence, I can tell you
how many, but why bother. It's none
of your business. Besides, they are going
berserk in there.
I am ever-changing…clumsy.

Wounded and bloodstained on my pale skin, there
is no cure for when the torpedo hits.
Blasting a union into war, I drown at the
mercy of a song.

I should have found shelter.
I take this suitcase with me,
remember my anguish…the love I
grabbed in haste.

IMPACT

I died on impact
when your heart slammed into mine
Hit and run
Pieces lodged
in skin, bones,
veins, muscle—anything for survival

How many eyes do you have?
You rush to find yourself but
never do

A fragment of heart still
attaches to you
Your brain thinks, veins suffer,
skull hurts, and your
soul reaches for nothing

Empty air goes through your nostrils
Blood leaps from your fingertips and you
are alone

ALONE

I am dead
You are quiet
They all are silent

Don't be tempted by
your throbbing heart to
join me
I lie motionless
beaching myself into your bones
There I will remain like any wife

Inside your sleep, your bones
will ache completely
We will be joined—
a new sex filling up with dreams

This is my dagger
Now I kill you back
In your mouth are teeth but in
your soul is nobody
This is what you get for not
coming with me

BLUE SKIES

Outside of our sphere, the world
is slow. You and I are like a
collection of half-hearted postcards one
just can't seem to throw away.

Here we are, still together in thoughts;
each with compelling tales and a
future patterned randomly—
victims to our own
painful recall.

There is a war in my brain. A treaty
is needed to characterize this conflict.

I am convinced of good things—
of life that is neither here nor there. It is
chilling to think of how serious
I am and how you are.
We don't see love; only feel it
rooted. I don't have children. I have been
faithful. This is the worst war in
my memory.

EMPTY FIELD

Today with flowers in
every room
for what doesn't matter
I am well aware
what you want
I am a monster
waiting...
mournful...

Wounded
my language penetrates
your eyes
You disperse your attention elsewhere

Sometimes when I sleep
I dream you love me
but when I'm awake your heart
fills with traffic

Each morning
you align yourself to perfection
but not me
I stand at this
window and silently
pound my fists
Your kiss could have been
light—
A child's secret—
deep and apart from
all others

All this camouflaging
worries me

The garden is dead
The shadows are single

PASSION

Do you really understand
being under the grass?

A terrible image,
too distinct
Even drinking can't make
it silly

Internationally, everyone
loves you.
Something is wrong

I like you
It is more terrible than
wonderful.
All these years beautifully
grating on ambivalent things,
getting deep and dragged
relentlessly into an explosion in
your mind.
So deep in fact
you killed yourself after
the baby's first kiss.

This poem is in memory
of you, abandoning me
and your guests

HARVEST

For Husband-Husband

He was sufficient in his
own little factory.
At exactly the same time, he'd
get up in the morning, write, and
eat a sub for dinner.
He'd even sweat on schedule.
I can't escape his breath.

If I could be read like the
rings on chopped down trees, one
would know the years of a hollow living,
a vision only for stars.

He was a constant death hovering
over my shoulder. A shadow I couldn't get rid of.
What if I stand in another
room? Is he gone? I turn and face
the sun, which burns my eyes, is this enough penance?

He got lost in himself.
A punctual time clock I couldn't
keep up with.
After all, factory work is
only piece work for the lonely.

The only moments
spent with me was in his dreams.
I am well now,
learning to awaken my voice.
The only screams heard are his
coming back to him.
The pores on his skin explode daily.
Real life, unattainable and sad.
I burned our pictures.
They are ash blowing up into
his stomach to give him worms.

IN HELL

My intuition says fetch a
piece of soul here—heart
bits once in awhile.
Is this a bad habit?

Come closer and speak to me.
I'm not your enemy until
you kiss me.
Then my bones circulate around
your heart and crush—
No one will assassinate you better.

Perhaps you think I'm crazy.
Don't be skeptical in your judgment.
Perhaps you think I've got
you cornered...
Perhaps I do.

Maybe I'm your protector
or murderer.
Don't be ridiculous:
I'm neither.

I only want one thing and that
is to see you fall to pieces—

SILENCE

At night, silence hits my heart
I can't sleep
You are one of those things that happened—
long-winded and exiled from my voice

In this darkness, my hands are cold—
like stone,
freezing with such paleness
Odd, you think I'd
be warm here in bed

The hours seem to pause
I wonder where your
moment was—
which hour or second that
has gone by killed you

When last I saw you, your hands and mouth
were uncomfortable—
revealing tales to memory
It rains slowly

I am tormented by this image and scarcely
know what to do with it
A landscape of muddy water and you
misleading me into another drowning
Well, my face is resurrected and there
is no grave here
Your ashes are beyond your
appearance

When I sleep in defenseless sheets, it
is not your soul I want to visit
It is not your smell I want to smell and
it is not your body I want to touch

In this dream, bit by bit you're
replaced so when dawn comes, my
heart cannot fly
I know the only portrait I need
to keep of you is in a drawer
buried by other arriving papers

ROUGH-EDGED

What did you expect from me?
Instead of falling naturally in love, we
were pushed, weak, and spooked.
It would be refreshing not to
be a failure. I'm tired of
having a controversial heart.

What happened?
I'm dramatic, cruel, and seldom pretty.
All this frustration is exhilarating and
demanding separation into pain and more pain.
And you in your state, hunting for
affection that was always there illustrates
your ability to cry for detail.
Will our story end in reconcile?

For better or worse, we kill when we love.
Bleed my body dry—maybe then I can
start over.
This tension doesn't have to pull us apart.
Dark visions can be recognized and with a
better mouth, you can manage to
kiss me.
In my own eyes, I remain fragments gluing
myself to wild hearts—
looking for love in volume.

OCEAN

It is morning
The light wanders onto
my walls...
into my internal love affair

My head shrinks
into the pillow again
I could not get up nor did
I like being a
human being today

Don't be sorry
The ocean is closer to
me than anyone else
The midst of new love
bonds prophesy
to my vision

The clouds knock
at the door
I get up
I go out

On the beach, I think how
a brain becomes
transparent
I breathe bitterly but
kiss me anyway
There is no escape

DESTRUCTION

We are nothing but bones wandering the earth
A living grave searching for marigolds
We want to separate our souls and lie down

All your experiences have been destruction
Your bones are brittle, splintered and rotten
detaching themselves to
pull at your heart

And me, I have many tears inside
They keep my heart moist—
My bones stay in place and catch these drops
One by one, they are offered to the stars
They will attach
themselves to light

And you, you wander and destroy yourself
over and over
I stop at times and watch, but am able to turn away
You can't slaughter me
You think of me often and wish you could
have caught a star in flight
Dream baby, because it will never happen
Your thoughts escape into the air and
disintegrate like ashes

BLOOD BRILLIANT

Glimpse this:
Perhaps you find me adorable...
Perhaps you see me as a widow...
Perhaps you feel me as blood-warm
and occasional...

Sooner or later you'll contain
my white heat.

You want me?
Breathe!
You love me?
Struggle!
You appreciate me?
Shut up!

I don't take flames.
You will have to suffice
this broken cord—

A KISS OF THE LIPS

How can I help you?
You are like a dog at
times, sucking up to my trail

Bones for pain
Bones for a quick exit

Fine
but I'm sad with arms in
a hurry
Brittle centuries have passed
Let my soul vanish into
sleep, long...
clearing heavy secrets...

Red, blue, maybe
some pink—
My being flows there
If you really want to know me
open a vein in front of
a mirror

A quiet voice will talk to you
It will comfort and love you
Its blood, sweet
like a kiss that never touches
your lips

Why? Because
thoughts are destroyed each year
Mine just manage to
escape, attaching themselves to
someone else, dying

PAIN

I hear pain coming from
every house on the street
Why is that so?
In that house on the corner
it is too late to arrive
They regret they have to
stay locked up
A friend of theirs died this hour
There are no children to cry
I will be their child
I will weep

Across the street in the
yellow house, there is no
mercy
They extinguish their hearts
with wind
It is four in the morning
They do not exist
Now, come into my house
I write a little poem
I claw, cry, and regret but I do
not move
I only write
I write more than ever
I owe my thoughts nothing
I give thanks—
I spread my brain apart and let
thoughts echo into the boundaries

The birds chirp and I'm sleepy
Today, if the wind lifts
my skirt
I will laugh
I will wander a different street and repeat
pain, dancing

QUIET SKY

The wind embraces my body
with fury
My hair will never
return to its original position
My hands can't get warm, and I
forgot where my gloves are
Memory freezes and falls
down by my feet

I can't speak now
Panic sets in and then I
see you
You with such sweet freedom, and me
with bursting pain, only my
eyelids could blink
You don't notice me
You are in another sky where
there is calm
A magic quietness that
no longer breathes

Standing here, waiting for a bus, it snows
Each flake is so full of depth—
tiny cubes of fallen hearts trying
to take mine

My mind starts to dance
The surface of my skin proclaims
an innocence
Once I knew what halos were and that
love travels into the abyss when it is true
My hands were warm then
Love was history in the making for
one moment

The snow turns to hail—
little pellets beating my
skin and reflecting my mistake

When the temperature rises, this will stop
The sky will be faithful somewhere on earth
I will keep walking into eternity to seek your dark
eyes softening my emptiness

Until then, I am a museum for the world
A fallen girl worshipped like Mary—
a martyr...lovely and waiting, swollen with
tears and prophetic images

I will watch silence and wait for
the wind to hurt your heart into an uncertainty

My spirit wants to be your
shadow even when there
is no sun, no clouds, no purpose, but just
a tenderness after a long struggle
When I saw you, I realized love wasn't
worth the sorrow
To my astonishment, there was an altar for hearts,
communion was weekly and somehow—
someday a new love, which was an old love,
would return

NOTHING DIVINE HERE

Precisely and efficiently
I shift my path towards you

Silence

I hear its voice...breaking...
softening up for death
I just can't face
its kiss—soundless
Is this what you wanted me to say?

Tonight, I tell myself its ok if
our love is white, hollow and terrified
After all, look what it dealt with

Oh heart, lock in some power—
but in a way that's innocent
like a skeleton found in an icebox

For me, sacrifice
For me, nothing
For me, false starts
If you let me, I'll pull
my heart out, all tainted with blood:

Tell me how you survived
The grief I feel, forgotten
Heart, come back and
just settle. Pass into
an understanding flesh can't remove

PART II

THE SAINT OF HEARTS

There are many rooms of sadness in
this world, I just happen to be
in one of them.

I thought about gathering all
the hearts of those I love and laying
them under my pillow.
I would be comforted this way.
The Virgin Mary throws back her
head and laughs.
She thinks this is a funny thing to do.

I am engulfed with the holy.

My heart will soon be under
someone else's pillow
comforting them.
I will lie there and empty my wings.
I will not be the Virgin Mary but a
saint who doesn't laugh.
I will point to the world and
blood will flow covering
all hope and tears in a crust.

SCENE OF THE CRUCIFIXION

For Clare

i

I won't praise myself
when I open my mouth, I'll just groan—
experience my throat asphyxiated and
dry with pain

One last thing: Don't blame me

Don't blame me for my
lost faith, sour hours, my
guilt—need I go on?

ii

In the yard, a statue surrounded
by little lights—
Intimacy. That's what I remember feeling
as I stared at it. Somewhere in the night
a dog barked, and I tried to ignore
its hissing smile, a dead-end mystery
that still haunts me

iii

I just can't figure out this relationship
I know there is no guarantee and you have
merit (so I regard you as a champion...intriguing...)
but I have to repeat:
Don't complicate me

Where is your passion,
your diary of last days?
Do I wake you when I offend? When I
ask you where you are?
I imagine you silent

or else laughing, collapsing into
meaningful fragments
all blood-red and original
(I don't want to drop dead and experience
you appearing only then—)

iv

Clare, three and a half,
looks up and sees you for the first time:
What a handsome man!

Like her, my speech to you
is a transaction, exposing whispers
You are a journey inside my eyelids

For her I hold the horizon
She awakes and reaches for a cloud
to make it kind. By midday, she sings and I am
left wondering:
Should I scotch tape my heart to
someone else's skeleton, align myself to a star
breezing in through doorways

RITES

A. I am a delightful angel, out of uniform
B. I am tenderness, a bad-tempered dog released into
life untied
(This is how you will understand me)

C. Forget about what you heard
D. Let go, Your eyelids have a
different landscape now, a portrait
of my most effective vehicle—
a dream

I have faith that you will love me
I'm going to give you a
connection and take over your heart
This isn't a trick
I just simply slipped into
your eyes—I am living now—
awkwardly...

E. Kiss me
I'm collecting your lips, willing them to
keep returning
F. I am your protector
G. Poison for human grace

LIFE AS A MECHANICAL LITERATURE PIECE

I am not some little machine that
just functions
I know how to argue and kiss
I know that every hour and everyday
has its moments

Surrounding myself with people, I know
someday, they will tell my story—What a risk!
I must talk adequately and express delight—
it must be full of drama

Ok, so I really know they will be silent
I will die nameless and faceless
Just another one of those poets who has
been published

As a result, I continue to welcome failure
with some surprises

I will not be a slave
My voice is strong
I have tasted life and death
At least grant my soul a messiah. As I watch
my funeral, I will see the past as a present condition
Eventually a door will open

PART III

CHINA, 1989

Murdered fabric—
blood of a giant turned
disruptive
A voyage of texts
as broken travel, kicking
the spectacle of bone back
to earth

All silent

Army, guns, jeeps:
a museum for
moonlight
Underneath it artificial
flowers, sickness
silently drifts toward hell

Together underground
they collect their choir
sing
make their nest

The lights are out

Someday, armored with flutes
you will have moments—
beautiful—
Shut your eyes
Have a dream bite you
Like a creature, it will lead you
past death, past those cities
to a world beautifully photographed
only by your eyes

VISITING ARTYOM

I tend to forget I have to get
past this obstacle
Like everyone, I abandon my nightmares and
disappear into the streets—
A strange country:
bulletproof glass separates me from
my love but I manage

What am I doing here?
Can I be your hero?--not retreating into despair but
subjecting myself to your
powerful finger-pointing:
Is it they who detached our
values?
Our love is infectious—
Violent in a good sense—
It surrounds the enemy and provokes them into
terrorizing, leaping, destroying

Sleep now
I command you to
Even though sleep is forbidden
safely we will do it
No anxiety, only a beating heart hijacked into safekeeping
For eight hours, forget

You know, this all could be just one big accident
All for nothing, just dead bodies lying there nameless and
homeless but gifted; still, we can turn
fate around—play out the strings into melody
instead of screams

IT HAS TO BE THIS WAY

I ask you not to talk
It doesn't matter
just listen
It is dangerous to breathe—
to shape the day into your
longing

Let's forget about the streets, our
country
Let's go to the butchers and buy
meat
I'll fix you a meal
We'll eat and be happy
We'll resurrect the dead with our laughter
Others will come to our house
we'll rebuild
From one to another the
spirit will fight

We gather in exile
We define mother
win freedom
heal
caution
With our blessings today
we stalk skulls and we
travel death

Four years later...

It is night out
Under the door rests
a flame
We are bone, stuck
to stars
We hurry
Love, strengthen yourself
for we are free

Emptiness is lying down
White flags hatch
Love, the wings have fallen
We are exhausted
I hold on to
God
I am convinced that
our tongues go
all the way to the moon

DOG DANCE

I see your skull veiled by a cloud
Eyelids sunk
Hands pressed on knees
Heart gone
A sight of secrets

In the distance, a dog is howling as the
sirens pass
Does this dog know what I don't?
Is he crying for the dead?

The dead are a miracle
In the cemetery, graves connect and a festival
of arms try to touch one another
Passerby's wave good-bye and the stone
reminds me of their daily labor (of how strong or
brave they were)

I think living is brave
Death is a release
The dog knows—heaven is nothing but a frill

REPUBLIC

I will assassinate you, disarm
your soul and you will enter a
world of reluctance
This entitles you to nothing and
no one will give you passage
to dreams
You blew out the candles of
our people
Sacrificed our hearts
Burning them
to our skulls
All this blood for symbolism
Guerillas shoot and we
become extinguished
This is not a mundane war
Negotiations affirm you
made us prisoners
I am a prisoner fermenting
Assemble your republic and drink

LOWER ME

For Svetlana Dobritchinin

All my nights here, are like galleries.
I see different tones of darkness.
I've only been here 49 years, and already
I've been mutilated.

My country doesn't love me.
Its silence is heated, sweaty, and exhausted.
To speak, would only be a memory of
what once was.
Most my friends go unnoticed with
eyes quiet.
There is no escape. No way to
overthrow this dictatorship.
We're all freefalling, looking for
comfort to save us from impact.

Growing up in a street of grayness,
feelings stay underground.
I can't heal certain pulses.
At night, in the distance, stars
hurled themselves into my eyesight.
Impact was an invitation to the coffin.

I will kill you with disappointment.
The spirit can be resilient, domestic, and trustworthy.
It took me a long time to perfect this smile.
This way I avoid infiltration.

Seeing the dead bodies, I know when
they were killed by their rate of decay.
This is all so systematic.
Seen and unseen graves, are something the
mourning walk on or by daily.

Maybe only dreams can live. When we sleep,
we're resurrected. If my heart were only
an image, this horror wouldn't exist.

The cruel soldiers giving me pain aren't really.
I will die quickly, but my dreams will
free me of all these wounds.

Witness after witness will
speak of the chaos to fulfill the buried.
From cheek to cheek, they will
find freedom on their tongue.
Come with me now.
I will show you a wall stained with blood.
Something all flesh inherits.

BURIED DEFINITION

Eventually every human gets
a bullet they can be proud of

If we wake up or scratch, we
become invisible
I have to tell you, our existence
is abstracted
ready for swallowing candles
You know, flames for vigils—
for an angry fix
in a panic of sidewalks

Such an elevator of guns breathing
together deciding who
to kill next

Mr. President:
Whose heart is beating?
Stop it!
Whose heart is giggling?
Ask it!

This is the price we pay for
shadows flying over our shoulders, our
fire escapes, through our windows
wanting more clouds

SCORCH

Look at me.
Comprehend what I
am saying because tomorrow
they will murder me.

This is a harsh reality.
All because I witnessed a crime on
the platform of the subway
station.

Don't think that you
can tell me what to do,
what to think, or when
to sleep.
Christ, I'm dissolving into
an emphasis of solitude.

I guess this was my fortune:
to be talented and not tell.
Everyone has dreams.
Mine last into the long hours
stabbing me despite my objections.
My compulsion is to go somewhere—
You are sentenced for a life of
continuous murder.

WHITE SHEET

1. DEATH

This war commutes through veins
spreading its tender game
Darkness is eternal, and love is
hidden behind hearts
No country will sentence itself to tears
We're all too respectable for that
Damn you!
We are hugging something deeper
than a body

2. WAR

With our eyes quiet, we weep
Looking at the soldier's bodies, they
seem only asleep with numb mouths
Speech is avoided
We are sad

3. THE FEAST

Write this down little fingers
Our bones are coded
One tibula painted red—an easy break non-chewable
One femur painted green—a home to crawl under
The remainder of bones are sacrificial
The ground needs some reminder
of skeleton

4. RESURRECTION

What is this? A miracle of heaven or fragments
of mistakes?
Some bones push up out of the casket,
out of the earth towards the sun
Flowers announce their presence in pastel colors—
a museum piece

The public gathers
Everyone is confused on this day
The sentence is on us now
Death from a compass that was false
We moved in the wrong direction
Our heart, our love, is forever vacant

5.   *AFTER*

Now sadness loves us
Pray for the bones in the cemeteries
Holy water is a vision stuck to this void
When we thirst for the earth, we will
exist for hands—they travel
our image to our soul
We will invent a quiet transaction that
only we can invent
Play it safe love, the final page
is free
Accept it

THIRD STREET

Fire can't witness
my flesh.
I refuse to recognize dark,
to identify with trembling.

A wet snow ticks.
Life as translucent
shirts, hanging in yards prepared
for terror.

The family in that yard
lost its son,
the family over there
is sad and so on.
This is why my ashes talk.
They blow from street to street
trying to escape, trying to evaporate
into sweat—

PART IV

DOPPELGANGER

i

I was born behind a moustache
Worst of all was my name
I know it sounds normal but I
can't forget the event
I dreamt of being a man and I am

The voice at night raising frustration at
work and crying on the sofa
Trying to free myself from my
chin
A thread to suffer
I remain living but actually I'm in
a deep death

A poor, poor, poor piece of dirt with
white eyes tired of pain and
objects
I won't dramatize but it's so
absurd and torn

At midpoint in my life
a machine noticed
and
twenty years later I'm a garden somewhere

ii

Walking through the hallway
door, I felt an artificial
presence
a warm execution taking me away
It was as if the postponement of death could
be no longer delayed
Clearly this frozen cluster has
gone out of its way to
cover me with blankets

What did I do to
deserve going so fast?
Was I born with hind legs, a
missing suitcase or
a changing mirror?

My arms feel stars
My legs feel taller
and
my face like a rope netting
around the doorway
shades me from the intruder

A silence is heard and
worst of all the more
I listen, the quieter it
becomes, creeping with its
imperial plate
which silently says eat

iii

It was never seen by my family
We were all too invisible to
catch a glimpse
From one room to another
we searched, from house to
house and from country to country we
continued to search
We focused entirely
on nothing else

We began to get light on
our feet, orphaning
the freedom we thought we had
wearing gaudy decorations
such honor we bestowed on
ourselves
Then, by our own default, the
music started
the reminiscence began
and
the labor of tears cried on shoulders

Our blood got thin and
our hearts submitted to
the upside down
This flute that we bore
was over

iv

This activity was dressed
in satin
Don't tell them that
This is their hats cutting off
their heads
These are ties from which they hang
Years later their bodies will lie
smelling of waterfalls and lilies

Take off your coat
Put on your shoe
My hand is over my eyes as I
watch you

The houses wash
in the lake
The military is shooting
stripping me into bags
No, I dreamt this
No, I dreamt of a blast in August

We die quickly
of extraordinary beauty
this sickness of power

v

Anchored in the lake is
my labor soaked and handcuffed

Living is a business
Something that becomes
impossible to deal with

I need a hand to take away
this sadness
this hostility of
forbidden aching

Four months ago, I wanted to
smuggle out of my life
throwing years of a shaky adventure
into a long sunrise

I know this is terrible but I
can laugh
It's winter
It's cold and this living
is surrender

vi

I go to my future now
good-hearted
whispering my arm is bare
Flesh for insects

In the yard with the
sky so boring
there is a low-keyed voice yelling
Orphan!

I waste no time
This experience is my best hour
with glittering bugs chewing until the heat
bursts my blood
Which one of us will last longer
my bones or their backs?

I fall apart
from love
I lived on the red
earth and embraced
happiness, slyfully not understanding
a thing

vii

I talk to myself in an
off key blush
my feet sinking endlessly
into the slaughter

My strength isn't astonishing
It is warm
I'm ashamed of myself for sentencing
my heart to such a prison

I want to spring forth and tell
my friends I'm sorry
Night now is panting on
my face
What can I say
My wrists are light and
I should have died years ago
but
my memory is carving
victory into my hands

PART V

AFTERMATH

Living on this earth is
one big nightmare.
This landscape frightens me.
Too much death.
Think about it.

I refuse to fall short of detail so
here it is:
Death of emotion
Death of love
Death of skin
Whiteness of bone
Come on, kidnap something remarkable!
View it in a cage.
Narrate its life then kill it.
I prepared myself for this sadness.

The world's mistakes are peeking into
my eyes taking over.
Let's have a ceremony in the heartland.
Is unhappiness life? If death shows some
coherence and generosity, sharpen your knives.
I'm going away to where I really belong.
To me, this is uplifting.

FEAST

My head glides in for
the feast—
invisible—
Every day my hands and my
destinies—
your eyes...

Oh, let me tell you—
It is a distinction
marking my birthplace.
You, my body, could scrape
only one cell,
a souvenir—

This age is pale.
I crane for the unbearable.
Look, I want atmosphere
with force—

So imagine wheels toward
my objective
and the tension a delivery,
a roll call saying love me—

TORNADO

The sky has many arms reaching
down for me.
With success, I escape.
Five arms touched down in Arkansas, and three
in Texas today.
From the porch, I watch one make its rounds.
I feel happy.
It fills me with such emotion, showing me
my most favorite desires—chaos and destruction.

Such a gray wonder alert to every
object and human. I think of religion.
This is God cleaning up all maternal possibilities.
Live with nothing so you will feel awakened.

As I take cover, I don't know if I'll
die from natures inside. Thinking about it, I
forgive myself for past mistakes.
I am unwrapping myself for its arm.
A sensation I'll feel for one moment. A great
unity. I've been hurled toward the infinite—
sun, stars, night, and planets....sucked up, as I
try to hold on. This is a mysterious feeling—opening
my memories, and my life suddenly being overheard
by everyone.

DENIED EMOTION

I glimpse my
own face
like a family gathering
where change is only
beneath the skin

What we all are thinking jumps
topic to topic
sucked out like a mosquito

This is unbearable
The power and sadness
My heart is a slave
adoring the prophetic

Descending, errant,
threads in
a small room crammed with faces

Eventually they dress up for
agony
and wander this earth
a family driven by
spinning space

COLD

Suppose there are fibers in
my heart moving at a
calm rate stacking up darkness—
How long until it consumes me?

Suppose a handful of my blood forms
into a voice—
a voice which light from the sky melts
into a quiet solace—
Is it too much to fall asleep?

In one dream, I dream of
winter, a house, and the smell
of spring. I swallow it like it
swallows me.
Outside, a man beckons me
to where our bodies play like children.

In another, grandfather is lying in
a palace while everyone digs
all around him...
But here I am life—
Here I am heart—
Give me an understanding
to love the air and not take
breath for granted—

Leaving my sorrow alone and
touching my wing...

CHOIR

Look into my eyes
See my charm
I can increase your
sleep into a story

My skin is honest
cascading into
power
A Friday night in
a dusty rural town

Authentic and easy
I spend my days calling
attention to this

"SOMEONE GOES CRAZY, AND IN THE END HE DIES. EVERYONE CAN IDENTIFY WITH IT."
                                        -Heinz Emighholz

I am not concerned with reality,
pursuing goals or appearing significant.
That's why viruses have chosen my body
as their universe.

I want to go to sleep. My dreams
last night threatened me, and I love these
traumatic moments. When I wake up, I
feel left out, like events of the day are drawn
by the hands of others. I have no control.
I just wait and wait to drift into ash.

I wish I could sort out a
sequel in which there could be some
sort of happy ending--that life wouldn't be
continuous battles with disease, war, and love...
I'm going to die perfect.
It's the only way...
and when I die, my last image
will be you left behind on
my retina.

I cannot escape acts of will.

IMAGES OF GRAVE

I climbed the stairs,
reached to feel a new height
with each step
This foolishness will end—

Balls of red, broken glass—
Blood puffing up like air
I imagine death this way
Images I want

This impression is lasting
The condition is need
To the average, it becomes
a question of sign
They think
The humor is understated
Wake-up!
Bones are cringing with
disaster and piece by piece they
attach themselves to the forbidden

BEATEN

The woman is dead
This is a terrible city
My existence is in stone

Was it me
alone in a crowd and no
one saying anything?
A wounded memory in
a corrupt life

I manage to steal away
to secret spots where the
gardens are pale and the fire's
in the distance
I manage to moan of eroded pasts
and helplessness

Here my blood is warm
I cannot understand streets or
people
When I go back to the
race with trees and the
silent swans, I realize only
one thing
Everything I am is a current
flowing on the hour

ZOO

I have to talk fast—
before the lights go
out

It is best you don't
see my speech in action
Its clumsy dry sentences with
no affection
Sad

Like the zoo animals
drawn out by living
A few scraps and
no ambition

My iced heart is a monster
You took away my material
My enchanted life
There are lessons to learn
from this little lecture I give
It is genuine

Keep the lights on

CUT

My eyes wait like a bone
for skin to embrace it.
They float in your wounds,
in your door, which only opens
for parting.

Pretend I am a book
feeding you.
I am here striking your heart
like something waking
the air, earth sinks under
your hand...

Dark waters wait
for a gift, for fever in my words.
What we didn't choose
waits for a lilac, an island,
a visit from a light wind...

EVENING

It was like a grand explosion—
circling
The windows were splattered
with a cloaked moon and I
sat stained within
this structure
The shape of things leaped
out
Each letter I
wrote was running
sweet of ravenous frenzy

You say it has been difficult—
this parting of repressed sleep
Come on!
Tell me why you never walk,
bring love, or vaguely turn to
see my breasts

This apartment is like a splinter
I sit alone, pale and struggling
I pursue the animals

Our life is chaotic—
face it:
bare squats with
half-opened expressions and a
figure that is orphaned

I feel memory on my back
Years later this probably will be natural

CONFIDENTIAL MEMO

Imagine my sensitive mind devout and
explosive
combining itself with your intensity.
We could be like tiny scratches—painful but
distinct, bruised and bleeding but stabilized—
victims to each other's denial.
I recall one afternoon when you
unarmed my soul and flung it—
killing me—mutilating my existence—
The evidence is all over me.

Will someone anyone just look at my face?
I mean look deeper seeing a stripped woman lost.
If anyone can go one step further and help me—
guard what identification I have left and remain
calm—I would be very happy.
You see, all I want is to feel what
one innocent human being feels like.
Convince me that my verdict in life is
worth reading out loud.

Someone anyone, align yourself to this
survivor—
I will proceed constantly to love you.
My soul is what weighs the evidence—
Your eyes will give me hope—

PART VI

BRIDGE

The angels are ripping our
bodies apart, they're butchering corpses.
Look, we can't conceal that our flesh is dying.
Insects multiply in our blood.
And if this isn't enough, we can't
talk about it.
Hands are shaky. We are afraid of
breaking down, becoming weak, and being
killed by pity.
Silence is better.
A slight wind touches us.
We can nourish ourselves with this.

There's no shame in saying nothing.
Silence is life—talk is only a wound.
No barricade here, just waiting for another part.
A different day which will happen when
we don't exist—
Please remember us tenderly…
Knock your head against a wall and
resurrect us.

MY SEIGE

No angel would come to
my defense.
I am a prisoner. My legs
can't flee.
I must attack this fate.

I live on a rotten earth. Even though
the climate is sincere, my heart is overcast.
Oh Angel, I threw stones into
the bitter water. When I'm more
awake, I'll drink from those dead waves, and
break this unsolved exile into autumn.

In the absence of love, the trees
embraced my pain. They are my keepsake.
Oh Angel, hear my thoughts…love me.
If you can't, reach in for my heart, and remove
it with pliers. Fling it up into the air.
I will taste your power and be
registered in life as a singing
bird hating seeds.

OH ANGEL

I won't despair your dismissal
Sometimes the roses change
Invisible in the darkness—that's
how I feel

Like a curtain hanging by
strings
I float
I look for one
who is delicate
who shines like a bulb

Please take me away from
the unacceptable

Look, I groan everyday
I have no interest except
to be heard

In the spring, I will
stand on solid ground
It's that easy—
a disentangled immersion
Don't try to comprehend what
I'm saying
This is not a pop quiz

My life is amateur
cruel at times
Oh Angel, why couldn't I
have practiced ahead of time
I don't know why your wings
caught on my brow

The only thing clear to
me is space
I ache
I look at my hands when

this happens

You hit me like vodka
I glimmer and beg for sky

Ten minutes from here a tour group
tours a lonely beach
An old woman praises her own
rosy cheeks
and me—
I hunt for a garden where
manuscripts are spoken

WILD

Oh Angel, at dawn,
I get up and sit in the nicest room.
I pour a cup of coffee and listen
to the birds.

The thing I love most
at this time: I feel life shivering
for life.
It knows at the slightest stoke, death
will take its friskiness and spit it
out.

I can't imagine not seeing the
fullness of the sun.
If the day does darken, can I
still sit in the nicest room?
I have an ugly room—quite messy.
Should I sit there and let
months pass?—
My stomach hungers for wind.
Feeling dust, I pack it
into my intestines.

GUARDIAN ANGEL SITS ON LEFT

The angel is curled against
me reduced.
I cannot ask to see her.
She protects me.
I cannot see her unhappiness
only my imbalance

I spoke to her of sadness…
I know this is terrible but I
still spoke.
Will the angel abandon me in
this struggle?
She tried to warn me of the
ripples breaking the adhesive.
I wouldn't listen.

Yesterday, bitterness engulfed me.
I was fearful.
Feeling bad, I threw white lilies all
over the living room floor.
An offering deposited…my heart resting below
those translucent petals.
The angel didn't respond.
I guess the barrier between us
left her chilly.

Oh Angel, what is needed?
How tragic I must seem.
The angel went on to guard another.
Guess she got tired of me.
My body embalms another void
and begs.

THE VACATIONING ANGEL

The vacationing angel deserted us
Swimming pools have become vivid graves—
tombs for God
Our bones, and skin are static—
trashed
In fact, if you haven't had plenty of dreams, you
will drop off this planet
One can't survive on knowledge

Hollow and silent, we are waiting
to die with a few pauses in-between
Nevertheless, we keep going
The trees have all grown thorns, and the
flowers are horizontal
We have no teeth to eat, and cannot
digest the bitter mass of voice

Vacationing angel, I don't blame you for
leaving
Come back! Wash these stains
Surround us with pockets of air so
we can embrace this slaughter

Oh Angel, this year has gone to pieces
The Sun never appeared

CAUTIONARY

I could have imagined many things—but
never you like this...
crushing down all love with your fist into
a small box which stays floating
through your veins.
Must I slice open a vein to get it?
What if I cut your neck when the box is
in your calf?

Love is complicated but necessary. When
I die, leaving you with memories is not good enough.
What if I open your small box and there is absolutely
nothing there? No documentation of the heart.

What if the small box is full of blood swirling in circles with
no way to stop until death?
Maybe death is the only true love we get.
Maybe death is just air and just maybe our decaying
bodies are solid earth for the insects, and love is
just a pact we have with dirt.

EVERY DEATH IS A MURDER

Dear maggots:

I hope you enjoy the chewing of flesh. Is 54
years difficult to swallow? My memories are stuck in
your stomach making you behave like me.
Pretty funny for a bug. What if you decide to
become a vegetarian? You know, I was one.

Do you like to lie down at night and look at the stars?
Or look at the blue sky if it is day?
My existence was a joke. God wanted me to
be your food. Will you spit out any part of
me you don't like and make a face?
Pretty funny for a bug.
Does flesh get caught if you take too big of a bite?

I should have drank more in my life. Instead, I did
everything good, disguised myself daily—
exploding into every hour bravely
speaking for what is right. My poetry is
butchered and bloody—its rage, my kiss—
a memento I leave this world.

Maggots, how many words will you have of mine?
Will I be strong in the Maggot world or
dissolve into weather? My bones, stuck to the
ground shivering, were crushed by the garbage truck.
Maggots, enjoy your little steak.
My blood, seeps into the ground with extraordinary flare.
I hope you live your life differently.

ABOUT THE AUTHOR

Gloria Mindock is the author of *La Porţile Raiului* (Ars Longa Press, 2010, Romania) translated into the Romanian by Flavia Cosma and *Blood Soaked Dresses* (Ibbetson Street Press, 2007). She is editor of Červená Barva Press and the *Istanbul Literature Review*, an online journal based in Istanbul, Turkey. She has had numerous publications including *Poet Lore*, *River Styx*, *Phoebe*, *Blackbox*, *Poesia*, *Bogg*, *Ibbetson*, *WHLR*, *UNU: Revista de Cultura*, *Citadela*, *Aurora*, *Arabesques*, and two chapbooks, *Doppelganger* (S. Press) and *Oh Angel* (U Šoku Štampa). From 1984-1994, Gloria was editor of the *Boston Literary Review/BLuR*. She has been nominated for a Pushcart Prize, St. Botolph Award, and was awarded a fellowship from the Massachusetts Cultural Council distributed by the Somerville Arts Council. Gloria currently works as a Social Worker and freelances teaching poetry workshops and editing manuscripts.

AUTHOR'S NOTE

When I first moved into the Boston area in 1984, I found that everywhere I went, people would tell me their problems. I expected to hear all sorts of problems and difficulties from my clients, but never from the general public. It seems like I could never get away from it. *Nothing Divine Here* is not about me or anyone I know except for one poem. This book is only an accumulation of all the stories I heard written in first person.